Climbing to the Top

A Guide to Success in Any Career

Millie Kiama

Copyright © 2024 Millie Kiama

All rights reserved

No part of this book may be reproduced, or stored in a retrieval system, or transmitted in any form or by any means, electronic, mechanical, photocopying, recording, or otherwise, without express written permission of the publisher.

Contents

Title Page
Copyright
Book Disclaimer
Introduction — 1
Chapter 1: Define Your Goals — 4
Chapter 2: Continuous Learning and Development — 7
Chapter 3: Cultivate Leadership Skills — 10
Chapter 4: Build a Strong Network — 13
Chapter 5: Embrace Challenges and Take Risks — 16
Chapter 6: Adaptability and Flexibility — 19
Chapter 7: Work-Life Balance and Well-Being — 22
Chapter 8: Lead by Example — 25
Chapter 9: Adapt and Evolve — 28
Chapter 10: Celebrate Achievements and Keep Moving Forward — 31
CLosing remarks — 34
About The Author — 37
Books By This Author — 39

Book Disclaimer

This book is for informational purposes only. Readers are encouraged to use their discretion and seek professional advice where appropriate. The author and publisher disclaim responsibility for action taken by readers based on the information presented in this book.

Introduction

The Path To Success

In today's fast-paced and competitive job market, achieving success in your career requires more than just talent and hard work. It demands strategic planning, continuous learning, adaptability, and a strong sense of purpose. Whether you're a recent graduate embarking on your professional journey or a seasoned professional aiming to ascend to new heights, navigating the path to success can be both exhilarating and challenging. However, with the right mindset, skills, and strategies, you can overcome obstacles and reach the pinnacle of your chosen career path.

Understanding the Competitive Landscape

The modern job market is characterized by rapid technological advancements, globalization, and ever-changing industry trends. As a result, professionals must constantly adapt to new challenges and opportunities in order to stay relevant and competitive. Understanding the dynamics of the job market and identifying emerging trends in your industry is essential for crafting a successful career strategy.

The Importance of Dedication and Perseverance

Achieving success in any field requires unwavering dedication and perseverance. It's important to set ambitious goals for yourself and commit to pursuing them with determination and resilience, even in the face of setbacks and obstacles. By maintaining a positive attitude and staying focused on your long-term objectives, you can overcome challenges and continue moving forward on your path to success.

Strategic Planning for Career Advancement

Success rarely happens by chance—it requires careful planning and strategic decision-making. Whether you're aiming for a promotion, seeking new opportunities, or starting your own business, it's crucial to develop a clear roadmap for achieving your career goals. This involves identifying your strengths and weaknesses, exploring potential career paths, and setting realistic milestones for your professional development.

Continuous Learning and Skill Development

In today's rapidly evolving job market, staying ahead of the curve requires a commitment to lifelong learning and skill development. Investing in education, training programs, and professional certifications can help you acquire new skills and stay abreast of industry trends. Additionally, seeking out mentorship opportunities and networking with industry professionals can provide valuable insights and guidance as you progress in your career.

Building a Strong Personal Brand

In a competitive job market, having a strong personal brand can set you apart from the competition and open doors to new opportunities. This involves cultivating a professional online presence, showcasing your expertise and achievements, and actively engaging with industry peers and thought leaders. By establishing yourself as a trusted authority in your field, you can attract new opportunities and advance your career more effectively.

Embarking on the path to success in your career is a journey that requires dedication, perseverance, and strategic planning. By understanding the competitive landscape, committing to continuous learning and skill development, and building a strong personal brand, you can navigate the challenges of the job market and achieve your professional goals. Whether you're just starting out in your career or aiming to advance to higher levels, remember that success is not a destination—it's a journey. With determination, resilience, and a clear vision of your goals, you can climb the ladder of success and reach new heights in your chosen career path.

Chapter 1: Define Your Goals

Establishing clear and specific career goals is the cornerstone of success in any profession. By defining your goals, you create a roadmap for your career journey and set yourself on a path towards achievement and fulfillment. In this chapter, we delve into the importance of goal-setting and provide practical strategies for identifying and pursuing your aspirations.

Understanding the Power of Goal Setting

At its core, goal setting is about envisioning the future you desire and taking proactive steps to make it a reality. By setting clear objectives for your career, you provide yourself with direction, motivation, and a sense of purpose. Goals serve as benchmarks for measuring progress and evaluating success, helping you stay focused and committed to your professional development.

Identifying Your Career Aspirations:

The first step in defining your goals is to reflect on your career aspirations and envision where you want to be in the future. Consider your passions, interests, and values, as well as your strengths, weaknesses, and areas for growth. What do you hope to achieve in your career? What impact do you want to make? By clarifying your aspirations, you can set meaningful and achievable goals that align with your vision for the future.

Setting SMART Goals

To ensure your goals are actionable and attainable, it's essential to follow the SMART criteria:

- Specific: Clearly define what you want to accomplish, avoiding vague or ambiguous objectives.

- Measurable: Establish concrete criteria for measuring progress and success, enabling you to track your advancement over time.

- Achievable: Set goals that are within your reach and feasible given your current circumstances and resources.

- Relevant: Ensure your goals are relevant to your overarching career objectives and contribute to your professional growth and development.

- Time-bound: Establish deadlines or timelines for achieving your goals, providing a sense of urgency and accountability.

Creating a Roadmap for Success

Once you've identified your career goals, it's time to develop a strategic plan for achieving them. Start by breaking down your objectives into smaller, actionable steps or milestones. Consider the skills, experience, and qualifications you need to reach your goals, and create a roadmap for acquiring them. This may involve pursuing additional education or training, gaining hands-on experience through internships or volunteer opportunities, or seeking mentorship and guidance from industry professionals.

Maintaining Flexibility and Adaptability

While it's important to set clear goals and develop a plan for achieving them, it's also essential to remain flexible and adaptable in the face of change. Your career path may evolve over time, and unforeseen challenges or opportunities may arise along the way.

Be open to adjusting your goals and strategies as needed, and embrace new opportunities for growth and development.

Defining your goals is the first step towards success in your career. By identifying your aspirations, setting SMART goals, creating a roadmap for success, and maintaining flexibility and adaptability, you can chart a course towards achievement and fulfillment in your chosen profession. Remember, your goals are not set in stone—they can evolve and change as you grow and develop in your career. Stay focused, stay motivated, and never lose sight of the vision you have for your future.

Chapter 2: Continuous Learning and Development

In an era marked by rapid technological advancements and evolving industry landscapes, the pursuit of continuous learning and development has become a cornerstone of success in any career. In this chapter, we delve into the importance of ongoing education and professional growth, and explore strategies for staying competitive and thriving in today's dynamic job market.

Embracing Lifelong Learning

The pace of change in the modern workplace is unprecedented, making it imperative for professionals to embrace a mindset of lifelong learning. By committing to continuous education and skill development, you not only stay relevant in your field, but also position yourself as a valuable asset to employers and clients. Whether it's mastering new technologies, acquiring industry-specific certifications, or honing soft skills such as communication and leadership, there are endless opportunities for growth and advancement through lifelong learning.

Investing in Ongoing Education

One of the most effective ways to stay competitive in your career is to invest in ongoing education and professional development.

This may involve enrolling in formal degree programs, attending workshops and seminars, or participating in online courses and training modules. By expanding your knowledge base and acquiring new skills, you enhance your value as a professional and increase your opportunities for career advancement.

Seeking Mentorship and Guidance

In addition to formal education and training, seeking mentorship and guidance from experienced professionals can provide invaluable support and insights as you navigate your career journey. Mentors, coaches, and industry experts can offer guidance, share their experiences, and provide constructive feedback to help you overcome challenges and achieve your goals. By building meaningful relationships with mentors and seeking their advice, you can accelerate your learning and development and gain valuable perspective on your career trajectory.

Networking and Collaboration

Networking with peers, colleagues, and industry leaders is another essential aspect of continuous learning and development. By participating in professional associations, attending networking events, and engaging with online communities, you can expand your professional network, exchange ideas, and stay informed about industry trends and best practices. Collaborating with others also provides opportunities for peer learning and knowledge sharing, fostering innovation and growth in your career.

Embracing Change and Adaptability

Finally, it's important to embrace change and maintain a mindset of adaptability as you pursue continuous learning and development. The world of work is constantly evolving, and the skills and knowledge that are in demand today may become obsolete tomorrow. By remaining flexible and open to new opportunities and challenges, you can position yourself for long-term success and thrive in an ever-changing job market.

Continuous learning and development are essential for staying competitive and thriving in today's fast-paced job market. By investing in ongoing education, seeking mentorship and guidance, networking with peers, and embracing change and adaptability, you can enhance your skills, expand your knowledge base, and position yourself for success in your career. Remember, the journey of learning is ongoing—embrace it with enthusiasm and curiosity, and let it propel you towards new heights of achievement and fulfillment.

Chapter 3: Cultivate Leadership Skills

In today's competitive professional landscape, the ability to lead effectively is not just a desirable trait—it's a critical component of career success. In this chapter, we explore the importance of cultivating leadership skills and provide actionable strategies for developing your abilities as a leader.

Understanding the Importance of Leadership

Leadership skills are essential for advancing to higher levels in any job or organization. Effective leaders possess the ability to inspire, motivate, and guide others towards common goals and objectives. They exhibit confidence, decisiveness, and emotional intelligence, and are capable of navigating complex challenges and driving positive change.

Developing Core Leadership Competencies

There are several core competencies that are essential for effective leadership. These include:

- **Communication:** Effective leaders are skilled communicators who can articulate their vision, ideas, and expectations clearly and persuasively. They listen actively, foster open dialogue, and communicate with empathy and respect.

- **Decision-Making:** Leaders must be able to make informed and timely decisions, even in high-pressure situations. They weigh risks and benefits, gather relevant information, and use sound judgment to arrive at effective solutions.

- **Motivation:** Inspiring and motivating others is a key aspect of leadership. Effective leaders understand what drives and motivates their team members, and they leverage this knowledge to foster a positive and productive work environment.

- **Problem-Solving:** Leaders are adept at identifying problems, analyzing root causes, and implementing solutions. They approach challenges with creativity and resourcefulness, and they encourage collaboration and innovation among team members.

Taking on Leadership Roles:

One of the most effective ways to develop leadership skills is to actively seek out opportunities to lead within your organization or community. This may involve taking on leadership roles in projects or initiatives, volunteering for committee positions, or serving in leadership capacities in professional associations or community organizations. By stepping up and taking on responsibility, you can gain valuable hands-on experience and demonstrate your leadership potential to others.

Seeking Mentorship and Guidance

Mentorship and guidance from experienced leaders can provide invaluable support and insights as you develop your leadership skills. Seek out mentors within your organization or industry who can offer advice, share their experiences, and provide constructive feedback on your leadership development. By learning from the experiences of others, you can accelerate your growth as a leader and avoid common pitfalls along the way.

Continuously Learning and Growing

Leadership is a journey of continuous learning and growth. As you progress in your career, invest in ongoing education and professional development opportunities to enhance your leadership skills and stay abreast of emerging trends and best practices. Attend leadership workshops, seminars, and conferences, and participate in leadership development programs offered by your organization or industry associations.

Cultivating leadership skills is essential for advancing to higher levels in any job or organization. By developing your ability to inspire and motivate others, communicate effectively, make sound decisions, and take on leadership roles, you can position yourself as a confident and capable leader in your field. Remember, leadership is not about a title or position—it's about the actions you take and the impact you have on others. Embrace opportunities to lead, seek out mentorship and guidance, and commit to continuous learning and growth as you strive to become the leader you aspire to be.

Chapter 4: Build a Strong Network

In today's interconnected world, building and maintaining a strong professional network is essential for career advancement and success. In this chapter, we explore the importance of networking and provide practical strategies for expanding and nurturing your professional connections.

Understanding the Power of Networking

Networking is more than just exchanging business cards or connecting on social media—it's about building meaningful relationships with individuals who can support, mentor, and advocate for you throughout your career journey. A strong network can provide valuable insights, advice, and opportunities for growth, as well as access to resources and information that can help you achieve your professional goals.

Cultivating Relationships

Effective networking begins with cultivating genuine, authentic relationships with colleagues, mentors, industry peers, and influencers. Take the time to get to know people on a personal level, and show genuine interest in their work and interests. Be proactive in reaching out to new contacts and maintaining existing connections, and look for ways to add value and support others in your network.

Attending Industry Events and Conferences

Industry events, conferences, and networking mixers provide valuable opportunities to expand your professional network and connect with key players in your field. Attend conferences, workshops, and seminars related to your industry or areas of interest, and take advantage of networking breaks and social events to meet new people and exchange ideas. Be prepared to introduce yourself and share information about your background, experience, and career goals, and follow up with contacts after the event to continue building relationships.

Utilizing Online Networking Platforms

In addition to in-person networking events, online networking platforms such as LinkedIn can be valuable tools for expanding your professional network. Create a compelling and professional LinkedIn profile that highlights your skills, experience, and accomplishments, and actively engage with others by sharing content, participating in group discussions, and reaching out to new connections. Use LinkedIn to research potential contacts, learn about industry trends, and stay connected with colleagues and peers.

Seeking Mentorship and Guidance

Mentorship is a powerful form of networking that can provide invaluable support and guidance as you navigate your career journey. Seek out mentors within your organization or industry who can offer advice, share their experiences, and provide feedback on your career development. Be proactive in seeking out mentorship opportunities, and be open to learning from the experiences of others.

Giving Back to Your Network

Networking is a two-way street, and it's important to give back to your network by offering support, advice, and opportunities for growth to others. Be willing to share your knowledge and expertise, make introductions, and offer assistance to those who may benefit from your guidance. By contributing to the success of others in your network, you strengthen your relationships and build goodwill that can pay dividends in the future.

Building a strong professional network is essential for career advancement and success. By cultivating genuine relationships, attending industry events and conferences, utilizing online networking platforms, seeking mentorship and guidance, and giving back to your network, you can expand your circle of contacts and access valuable opportunities and resources that can help you achieve your professional goals. Remember, networking is an ongoing process that requires time, effort, and genuine engagement—but the rewards of building a strong network are well worth the investment.

Chapter 5: Embrace Challenges and Take Risks

In the pursuit of success, one of the most critical factors is the willingness to embrace challenges and take risks. In this chapter, we explore the importance of stepping outside of your comfort zone, pushing boundaries, and embracing failure as a catalyst for growth and resilience.

Understanding the Value of Challenges and Risks

Success often lies on the other side of adversity. By embracing challenges and taking calculated risks, you open yourself up to new opportunities for growth, learning, and advancement. Whether it's pursuing a new career path, launching a business venture, or tackling a difficult project, stepping outside of your comfort zone is essential for personal and professional development.

Pushing Beyond Your Limits

To achieve your full potential, it's essential to push yourself beyond your perceived limits and boundaries. This may involve taking on tasks or projects that feel daunting or intimidating, or pursuing opportunities that stretch your skills and abilities. By challenging yourself to reach higher and aim for more ambitious goals, you can unlock hidden talents and capabilities that you never knew you possessed.

Embracing Failure as a Learning Opportunity

Failure is an inevitable part of the journey to success—but it's also one of the most valuable teachers. Rather than viewing failure as a setback or a sign of incompetence, embrace it as a learning opportunity and a stepping stone on the path to success. Analyze your mistakes, identify areas for improvement, and use setbacks as fuel for growth and resilience. Remember, every failure brings with it valuable lessons and insights that can inform your future decisions and actions.

Taking Calculated Risks

While taking risks involves a degree of uncertainty and potential for failure, it's essential to approach risk-taking in a strategic and calculated manner. Evaluate the potential risks and rewards of any decision or action, and weigh them against your long-term goals and objectives. Take calculated risks that have the potential to propel you forward in your career or personal life, but be prepared to adapt and pivot if things don't go as planned.

Building Resilience and Grit

Resilience—the ability to bounce back from setbacks and adversity—is a key characteristic of successful individuals. Cultivate resilience by developing a growth mindset, maintaining a positive attitude in the face of challenges, and seeking support from mentors, colleagues, and friends during difficult times. Build grit—the perseverance and passion to pursue long-term goals despite obstacles—by staying focused on your objectives and refusing to give up in the face of adversity.

Embracing challenges and taking risks are essential components of the journey to success. By stepping outside of your comfort zone, pushing beyond your limits, embracing failure as a learning opportunity, taking calculated risks, and building resilience and grit, you can unlock your full potential and achieve your goals. Remember, the path to success is not always smooth or easy—but by facing challenges head-on and taking risks, you can overcome obstacles and reach new heights of achievement and fulfillment in your personal and professional life.

Chapter 6: Adaptability and Flexibility

In the ever-evolving landscape of the modern workplace, adaptability and flexibility are not just desirable traits—they are essential for thriving amidst change. In this chapter, we delve into the significance of embracing adaptability and flexibility, and offer strategies for cultivating these qualities to stay ahead in today's dynamic work environment.

Understanding the Importance of Adaptability

The pace of change in the workplace is accelerating at an unprecedented rate, driven by technological advancements, shifting market trends, and global disruptions. In such a dynamic environment, the ability to adapt quickly and effectively is critical for success. Adaptability enables individuals and organizations to navigate uncertainty, seize new opportunities, and thrive in the face of adversity.

Embracing Change and Innovation

Rather than fearing change, successful professionals embrace it as an opportunity for growth and innovation. Be open to new ideas, technologies, and ways of working, and embrace change as a catalyst for progress. Stay informed about emerging trends and developments in your industry, and be proactive in seeking out opportunities to innovate and evolve.

Continuous Skill Development

To remain adaptable in a rapidly changing world, it's essential to continuously develop and update your skills. Stay abreast of advancements in your field, and invest in ongoing education and training to expand your knowledge and expertise. Develop a growth mindset that thrives on learning and improvement, and be willing to step out of your comfort zone to acquire new skills and competencies.

Cultivating Resilience in the Face of Challenges

Adaptability is closely linked to resilience—the ability to bounce back from setbacks and adversity. Cultivate resilience by maintaining a positive attitude in the face of challenges, seeking support from colleagues and mentors, and focusing on solutions rather than dwelling on problems. Approach setbacks as opportunities for growth and learning, and use them as motivation to push forward and overcome obstacles.

Pivoting When Necessary

In today's fast-paced world, it's essential to be willing to pivot and change course when necessary. Be open to feedback and constructive criticism, and be willing to reevaluate your strategies and approaches in light of new information or changing circumstances. By remaining flexible and agile, you can adapt to shifting priorities and seize new opportunities as they arise.

Adaptability and flexibility are essential qualities for success in today's dynamic work environment. By embracing change, continuously developing your skills, cultivating resilience, and being willing to pivot when necessary, you can stay ahead of the curve and thrive amidst uncertainty. Remember, adaptability is not just about reacting to change—it's about proactively embracing it as an opportunity for growth and innovation. By fostering a mindset of adaptability and flexibility, you can position yourself for success in any endeavor.

Chapter 7: Work-Life Balance and Well-Being

Amidst the pursuit of professional success, it's imperative not to neglect one's well-being and the balance between work and personal life. In this chapter, we delve into the significance of maintaining a healthy work-life balance and prioritizing well-being, and provide actionable strategies for achieving harmony in both aspects of life.

Understanding the Importance of Work-Life Balance

Achieving success in your career is undoubtedly important, but it should not come at the expense of your well-being and personal life. A healthy work-life balance is essential for overall happiness, fulfillment, and productivity. It enables individuals to recharge, rejuvenate, and maintain perspective, ultimately leading to greater job satisfaction and longevity in one's career.

Prioritizing Physical and Mental Health

To maintain a healthy work-life balance, it's crucial to prioritize both physical and mental health. Take regular breaks throughout the workday to stretch, move, and recharge. Incorporate physical activity into your routine, eat nutritious meals, and prioritize sleep to ensure optimal well-being. Additionally, prioritize mental health by practicing self-care activities such as meditation, mindfulness, or hobbies that bring you joy and relaxation.

Setting Boundaries and Managing Time Effectively

Establishing clear boundaries between work and personal life is essential for maintaining balance and preventing burnout. Set specific work hours and stick to them, avoiding the temptation to constantly check emails or work outside of designated times. Communicate your boundaries to colleagues and supervisors, and prioritize tasks based on importance and urgency to manage your time effectively.

Engaging in Activities that Recharge and Rejuvenate

Incorporate activities into your routine that help you relax, unwind, and recharge outside of work. Whether it's spending time with loved ones, pursuing hobbies and interests, or enjoying nature, make time for activities that bring you joy and fulfillment. Cultivate a sense of balance by dedicating time to both work and leisure, and recognize that investing in your well-being ultimately enhances your performance and effectiveness in all areas of life.

Fostering a Supportive Work Environment

Employers play a crucial role in promoting work-life balance and well-being within the workplace. Foster a supportive and inclusive work environment that values diversity, equity, and inclusion, and prioritizes the well-being of all employees. Offer flexible work arrangements, such as telecommuting or flexible hours, to accommodate the diverse needs and preferences of employees. Provide resources and support for mental health and wellness initiatives, and encourage open communication and feedback to address concerns and promote a positive organizational culture.

Achieving success in your career requires more than just professional accomplishments—it requires maintaining a healthy work-life balance and prioritizing your well-being. By taking care of your physical and mental health, setting boundaries between work and personal life, engaging in activities that recharge and rejuvenate you, and fostering a supportive work environment, you can achieve greater harmony and fulfillment in both your professional and personal life. Remember, success is not just about what you accomplish—it's also about how you live your life and the impact you have on others. By prioritizing well-being and balance, you can lead a more fulfilling and meaningful life, both in and out of the workplace.

Chapter 8: Lead by Example

As you ascend the ranks of your career, assuming leadership positions comes with a profound responsibility to lead by example. In this chapter, we explore the significance of setting a positive example, inspiring others, and driving meaningful change within your organization and industry.

Setting the Standard

As a leader, your actions speak louder than words. Lead by example by embodying the values and principles you wish to instill in others. Demonstrate integrity, professionalism, and ethical conduct in all your interactions, and hold yourself to the highest standards of excellence and accountability. By setting a positive example, you inspire trust, respect, and admiration among your colleagues and followers.

Mentoring and Advocacy

One of the most impactful ways to lead by example is through mentorship and advocacy. Take an active role in supporting and developing the talents of your colleagues, offering guidance, feedback, and encouragement along their career paths. Be an advocate for diversity and inclusion initiatives, championing the voices and perspectives of underrepresented groups and fostering a culture of belonging and respect within your organization.

Creating a Culture of Excellence

As a leader, you have the power to shape the culture of your organization. Cultivate a culture of excellence by fostering innovation, collaboration, and continuous improvement. Encourage a growth mindset among your team members, empowering them to take risks, learn from failures, and strive for excellence in everything they do. Celebrate achievements and recognize individuals who embody the values and behaviors that contribute to a culture of excellence.

Driving Positive Change

Use your position of influence to drive positive change within your organization and industry. Lead by example in advocating for social responsibility, sustainability, and ethical business practices. Take bold initiatives to address systemic issues and promote positive social impact, both within your organization and in the broader community. By leveraging your influence and resources, you can make a meaningful difference and leave a lasting legacy that inspires future generations of leaders.

Leading by example is not just a responsibility—it's a privilege and an opportunity to make a lasting impact on the world around you. As you climb the ranks in your career, remember the importance of setting a positive example, inspiring others, and driving meaningful change. By embodying the values of integrity, mentorship, excellence, and social responsibility, you can create a legacy that transcends your individual accomplishments and inspires others to reach their full potential. Lead with purpose, passion, and conviction, and leave a lasting imprint on the world as a leader who leads not only with words, but with actions.

Chapter 9: Adapt and Evolve

In the journey towards success, the ability to adapt and evolve is paramount. This chapter delves into the importance of resilience, flexibility, and embracing change as essential components of navigating the complexities of professional life.

Embracing Resilience in the Face of Challenges

Setbacks and challenges are an inherent part of any journey towards success. To thrive amidst adversity, cultivate resilience—the ability to bounce back from setbacks stronger than before. View challenges as opportunities for growth and learning, and maintain a positive mindset even in the face of adversity. Draw upon your inner strength and determination to persevere through difficult times, knowing that every obstacle you overcome brings you one step closer to your goals.

Remaining Adaptable in a Dynamic Environment

In today's fast-paced world, the only constant is change. Stay agile and adaptable by embracing change as an opportunity for growth and innovation. Be open to new ideas, technologies, and ways of working, and be willing to pivot and adjust your strategies as needed. Adaptability allows you to navigate shifting circumstances with grace and resilience, ensuring that you remain flexible and responsive to the demands of your environment.

Using Adversity as a Catalyst for Growth

Adversity has the power to transform us, if we allow it. Instead of viewing setbacks as roadblocks, see them as opportunities for personal and professional development. Reflect on the lessons learned from each challenge you face, and use them to fuel your growth and evolution. Adversity builds character, resilience, and wisdom, ultimately making you stronger and more capable of overcoming future obstacles.

Embracing Change as an Opportunity for Innovation

Change is not something to be feared—it is the catalyst for progress and innovation. Embrace change as an opportunity to innovate, experiment, and explore new possibilities. Be proactive in seeking out opportunities for growth and improvement, and be willing to challenge the status quo in pursuit of excellence. By embracing change with an open mind and a spirit of curiosity, you position yourself as a leader and innovator in your field.

The path to success is not a straight line—it is a journey filled with twists, turns, and unexpected detours. To navigate this journey successfully, cultivate resilience, adaptability, and a willingness to embrace change. View setbacks as opportunities for growth, and use adversity as a catalyst for personal and professional development. By remaining agile, resilient, and open-minded, you can adapt to any challenge or circumstance that comes your way, ensuring that you continue to evolve and thrive on the path towards success.

MILLIE KIAMA

∞∞∞

Chapter 10: Celebrate Achievements and Keep Moving Forward

In the final chapter of our journey towards success, we explore the importance of celebrating achievements and maintaining momentum as you progress in your career. It's essential to pause, reflect, and acknowledge the milestones you've reached, while also remaining focused on the future and the opportunities that lie ahead.

Recognizing and Celebrating Milestones

As you achieve milestones and reach new heights in your career, it's important to take time to celebrate your accomplishments. Whether it's landing a new job, completing a challenging project, or earning a promotion, each success represents a significant step forward on your journey towards your goals. Celebrate these milestones with gratitude, acknowledging the hard work, dedication, and perseverance that got you to where you are today. Share your achievements with colleagues, friends, and loved ones, and take pride in your accomplishments.

Maintaining Humility and Hunger

While it's important to celebrate achievements, it's equally important to remain humble and hungry for continued growth and success. Stay grounded in your values and principles, and never lose sight of the lessons you've learned along the way. Recognize that success is not just about reaching a destination—it's about the journey itself, and the continuous process of learning and development. Stay hungry for knowledge, experiences, and opportunities to challenge yourself and expand your horizons.

Embracing Lifelong Learning and Growth

Success is not a destination—it's a journey of continuous growth and self-improvement. Stay eager to learn, grow, and evolve in your career, and embrace opportunities for ongoing education and professional development. Cultivate a growth mindset that thrives on curiosity, innovation, and lifelong learning, and be open to new ideas, perspectives, and experiences that broaden your horizons and deepen your understanding of the world.

Staying Focused on Passion and Purpose

As you navigate your career journey, it's essential to stay connected to your passion and purpose—the driving forces that inspire and motivate you to excel. Remember why you chose your career path in the first place, and stay true to your values, interests, and aspirations. Let your passion fuel your ambition, and let your purpose guide your actions as you strive to make a meaningful impact in your chosen field.

As you celebrate achievements and milestones in your career, remember to keep moving forward with humility, hunger, and a commitment to lifelong learning and growth. Stay focused on your passion and purpose, and let them guide you as you continue to pursue excellence in your professional endeavors. Celebrate the journey, embrace the challenges, and never lose sight of the limitless potential that lies within you. With dedication, perseverance, and a relentless pursuit of excellence, the possibilities for success are endless.

Closing remarks

Your Journey to Success

As we conclude our exploration of the path to success, it's evident that reaching the pinnacle of your chosen career requires a multifaceted approach and unwavering commitment. Throughout this journey, you've discovered the key principles and strategies that can propel you towards your goals and help you stay there.

Defining Your Goals

Your journey begins with a clear vision of where you want to go. By defining your goals—both short-term and long-term—you set a roadmap for success and give yourself direction and purpose.

Investing in Continuous Learning and Development

In a world that's constantly evolving, continuous learning is essential for staying relevant and competitive. By investing in your own growth and development, you expand your skill set, broaden your knowledge base, and position yourself as a valuable asset in any job.

Cultivating Leadership Skills

Leadership is not just about holding a title—it's about inspiring others, driving positive change, and making a meaningful impact.

By cultivating your leadership skills, you empower yourself to lead by example and influence those around you towards success.

Building a Strong Network

No one achieves success alone. Building a strong network of mentors, colleagues, and supporters provides you with valuable guidance, support, and opportunities for growth.

Embracing Challenges and Taking Risks

Success often requires stepping outside of your comfort zone and taking calculated risks. By embracing challenges and seizing opportunities for growth, you expand your horizons and unlock your full potential.

Prioritizing Work-Life Balance and Well-Being

Maintaining a healthy work-life balance is essential for sustaining long-term success and well-being. By prioritizing self-care and setting boundaries, you ensure that you have the energy and resilience to pursue your goals with passion and purpose.

Leading by Example

As you ascend the ranks in your career, lead by example and inspire others to reach their full potential. By embodying the values of integrity, excellence, and accountability, you create a culture of success and empower those around you to thrive.

Adapting and Evolving

In a world of constant change, adaptability is key to staying ahead of the curve. By embracing change as an opportunity for growth and innovation, you position yourself for success in any job and industry.

Celebrating Achievements

Along the way, don't forget to celebrate your achievements and acknowledge the hard work and dedication that got you there. By taking time to reflect and celebrate your successes, you renew your motivation and inspire yourself to keep pushing forward.

As you embark on your journey to success, remember that the road may be challenging at times, but with perseverance, determination, and a clear vision of your goals, you can overcome any obstacle and achieve your dreams. Best of luck on your journey, and may you reach the pinnacle of your career with confidence and fulfillment.

About The Author

Millie Kiama

Millie Kiama, also known by her pen name Misty Miracle, is an accomplished author and dedicated educator hailing from a small town in Kenya. With a passion for both storytelling and nurturing young minds, Millie's journey has taken her from the shelves of her local library to classrooms and boardrooms around the world.

In addition to her role as a Resource teacher in Texas, where she cultivates a love for literature and creative expression among her students, Millie boasts over 15 years of experience in the banking and finance sector. She honed her expertise working for two of the world's major banking corporations, gaining invaluable insights into financial matters that complement her literary pursuits.

Beyond her professional endeavors, Millie is a staunch advocate for women and children, passionately supporting their empowerment and advancement. Her books, under both her given name and her pseudonym, Misty Miracle, reflect her diverse interests and talents, offering readers inspiration, guidance, and entertainment across various genres.

Millie's journey from humble beginnings to multifaceted success exemplifies the transformative power of perseverance and imagination. Through her writing and teaching, she continues to inspire others to explore the realms of fiction and self-discovery, inviting all to join her on a journey of enlightenment through the written word.

Books By This Author

Mastering Time: The Ultimate Key To Success

Thrifty Living: A Comprehensive Guide To Budgeting And Living Well On A Dime

Money Money Money: A Practical Guide To Financial Freedom

Mastering Negotiation: The Art Of Walking Away

The Path Of Success: Unveiling The Habits Of Highly Successful People

www.ingramcontent.com/pod-product-compliance
Lightning Source LLC
Chambersburg PA
CBHW072021230526
45479CB00008B/315